First World War
and Army of Occupation
War Diary
France, Belgium and Germany

15 DIVISION
45 Infantry Brigade
Royal Scots Fusiliers
7th Battalion
28 March 1915 - 5 May 1916

WO95/1947/1

The Naval & Military Press Ltd
www.nmarchive.com
Published in association with The National Archives

Published by

The Naval & Military Press Ltd

Unit 10 Ridgewood Industrial Park,

Uckfield, East Sussex,

TN22 5QE England

Tel: +44 (0) 1825 749494

www.naval-military-press.com

www.nmarchive.com

This diary has been reprinted in facsimile from the original. Any imperfections are inevitably reproduced and the quality may fall short of modern type and cartographic standards.

© Crown Copyright
Images reproduced by permission of The National Archives, London, England, 2015.

Contents

Document type	Place/Title	Date From	Date To
Heading	1947/1 7 Battalion Royal Scots Fusiliers.		
Heading	15 Division 45 Brigade 7 Bn Royal Scots Fus 1915 July-1916 Apr.		
Heading	15th Division 7th Royal Scots Fusiliers Vol. I 5-31-7-15 Jan 18		
War Diary	Chisledon	05/07/1915	08/07/1915
War Diary	Southampton	09/07/1915	09/07/1915
War Diary	Horse	10/07/1915	10/07/1915
War Diary	Boulogne	11/07/1915	11/07/1915
War Diary	Chisledon	09/07/1915	09/07/1915
War Diary	Folkestone	09/07/1915	09/07/1915
War Diary	Boulogne	09/07/1915	09/07/1915
War Diary	Folkstone	09/07/1915	09/07/1915
War Diary	Boulogne	10/07/1915	10/07/1915
War Diary	Boulogne (Ostrohove Camp)	10/07/1915	10/07/1915
War Diary	Audruicq	10/07/1915	10/07/1915
War Diary	Nortleilinghem	10/07/1915	15/07/1915
War Diary	Wallon-Capell	15/07/1915	16/07/1915
War Diary	Hamen Artois	16/07/1915	16/07/1915
War Diary	Hesdigneul	17/07/1915	31/07/1915
Heading	15th Division 7th Royal Scots Fusiliers Vol. II From 1-31.8.15		
War Diary	Hesdigneul	01/08/1915	03/08/1915
War Diary	Philosophe	03/08/1915	10/08/1915
War Diary	Quality Street	10/08/1915	18/08/1915
War Diary	Le Philosohe	18/08/1915	18/08/1915
War Diary	Mazingarbe	18/08/1915	29/08/1915
War Diary	Quslik Street	30/08/1915	01/09/1915
Heading	7th Battn. The Royal Scots Fusiliers. September 1915		
War Diary	Quality Street	01/09/1915	07/09/1915
War Diary	Noeux Les Mines	08/09/1915	18/09/1915
War Diary	Labeuvriere	19/09/1915	22/09/1915
War Diary	Vaudricourt	23/09/1915	25/09/1915
War Diary	Hill 70	26/09/1915	26/09/1915
War Diary	Noeux Les Mines	27/09/1915	27/09/1915
War Diary	Haillicourt	28/09/1915	29/09/1915
War Diary	Bruay	30/09/1915	01/10/1915
Map	English Miles		
Miscellaneous			
Map	La Bassee		
Heading	15th. Division 7th R. Scots Fusiliers. Vol 4 Oct 15		
War Diary	Bruay	01/10/1915	01/10/1915
War Diary	Labuissiere	02/10/1915	03/10/1915
War Diary	Allouagne	04/10/1915	12/10/1915
War Diary	Haillicourt	13/10/1915	14/10/1915
War Diary	Mazingarbe	15/10/1915	18/10/1915
War Diary	Trenches	19/10/1915	26/10/1915
War Diary	Noyelles	27/10/1915	31/10/1915
Heading	15th Division 7th R.S. Fusiliers Vol 5 121/7656		
War Diary	Noyelles	01/11/1915	03/11/1915

War Diary	Trenches	04/11/1915	13/11/1915
War Diary	Noeux	14/11/1915	18/11/1915
War Diary	Trenches	19/11/1915	24/11/1915
War Diary	Noyelles	25/11/1915	28/11/1915
War Diary	Trenches	29/11/1915	30/11/1915
War Diary	Verquin	01/12/1915	06/12/1915
War Diary	Trenches	07/12/1915	09/12/1915
War Diary	Sailly La Bourse	10/12/1915	11/12/1915
War Diary	Trenches	12/12/1915	14/12/1915
War Diary	Lillers	15/12/1915	31/12/1915
Heading	7th Royal Scots Fusiliers. January 1916		
War Diary	Lillers	01/01/1916	16/01/1916
War Diary	Mazingarbe	17/01/1916	31/01/1916
Heading	7th R. Scots Fus 15th Div Vol. 8 January 1918		
War Diary	Noeux	01/02/1916	06/02/1916
War Diary	Trenches	07/02/1916	18/02/1916
War Diary	Noeux	19/02/1916	29/02/1916
Heading	7th Royal Scots Fusiliers March 1916		
War Diary	Trenches	01/03/1916	17/03/1916
War Diary	Philosophe	18/03/1916	19/03/1916
War Diary	Trenches	20/03/1916	24/03/1916
War Diary	Noeux	25/03/1916	26/03/1916
War Diary	Apunoy	27/03/1916	27/03/1916
War Diary	Lapugnoy	28/03/1915	31/03/1915
Heading	7th Royal Scots Fusiliers. April 1916		
War Diary	Lapugnoy	01/04/1916	27/04/1916
War Diary	Bethune	28/04/1916	03/05/1916
War Diary	Vermelles	04/05/1916	05/05/1916

1947/1
7 Battalion Royal Scots
Fusiliers

15 DIVISION

45 BRIGADE

7 BN ROYAL SCOTS FUS

1915 JULY — 1916 APR

Amalgamated with 6 BN from
27 BDE 9 DIV to 45 BDE 15 DIV

AND KNOWN AS 6/7 BN from
1916 MAY WITH 15 DIV 45 BDE

MAPS/PLANS
RECORDED

45
15th Division

7th Royal Scots Fusiliers
Vol: I. 5—31.7.15.

Jan '16

I.F.

WAR DIARY or INTELLIGENCE SUMMARY.

Army Form C. 2118.

7th Royal Scots Fusiliers

Instructions regarding War Diaries and Intelligence Summaries are contained in F.S. Regs., Part II. and the Staff Manual respectively. Title pages will be prepared in manuscript.

(Erase heading not required.)

Place	Date	Hour	Summary of Events and Information	Remarks and references to Appendices
Chiseldon	1915 July 5th	6.45 pm	Received orders to embark for active service in France 6.45 pm	App +
"	8th		Transport proceed ball'n in advance - left Chiseldon at 3 a.m. entrained at SWINDON 8.10 a.m. Consisting of 3 officers - 108 r & f of Battalion and 5" attached.	
Southampton	9th		arrived Southampton 11 a.m. left Southampton 4.30 p.m.	
Havre	10	8 a.m	Transport disembarked HAVRE and entrained	
Boulogne	11	3.30	arrival BOULOGNE where the Battalion joined the Train	
			"	
Chiseldon	9th	3.5 pm	1st Train containing 16 officers (including 1 Brigade Chaplain) 450 other ranks left CHISELDON	
"		4.10 pm	2nd Train containing 13 officers and 436 other ranks left CHISELDON	
Folkestone		9.45 pm	1st Train arrived FOLKESTONE W and embarked at once on the S.S. INVICTA on which was already embarked the 13th & 15th Royal Scots	
Boulogne		10.5-5 pm	Disembarked and marched to Rest Camp at OSTROHOVE at which it arrived 12 midnight	
Folkestone		10.5 pm	2nd Train arrived FOLKESTONE ## and embarked on the ?	
Boulogne	10th	12.4N a.m	2nd Train arrived BOULOGNE, disembarked and marched to Camp OSTROHOVE at which it arrived 1.10 a.m	

A.H. Allenby Lt.Col
Comdg 7th R.S.F.

1577 Wt. W10791/1773 500,000 1/15 D. D. & L. A.D.S.S./Forms/C. 2118.

WAR DIARY

INTELLIGENCE SUMMARY.

7th B" Royal Scots Fusiliers Army Form C. 2118.

Instructions regarding War Diaries and Intelligence Summaries are contained in F. S. Regs. Part II. and the Staff Manual respectively. Title pages will be prepared in manuscript.

(Erase heading not required.)

Place	Date	Hour	Summary of Events and Information	Remarks and references to Appendices
BOULOGNE (OSTROHOVE Camp)	July 10	—	nil. nil.	
"	11	12.10 pm	Left camp by Rail and marched to PONT DE BRIQUE Railway station and entrained	
AUDRUICQ	11	6.10 am	Arrived here detrained and marched to NORTLEULINGHEM.	
NORTLEULINGHEM	"	8.30 am	Arrived, and went into Billets	
"	12	—	nil. nil.	
"	13	—	nil. nil.	
"	14	7.40 pm	Orders received for march to WALLON CAPEL - (Operation order B.E.F.) no. 13.7.15"	Appx 1
"	15	6.45 AM	Passed Starting point	
"	15	2.45 pm	Arrived at WALLON CAPELL	
WALLON-CAPELL	15	5.30	Received orders for March no. 16 5.7.15 - 15 HAM-EN-ARTOIS	Appx 2
"	16	8.15	Marched for HAM EN ARTOIS	
HAM EN ARTOIS	"	1 am	Arrived at destination and went into Billets at LE CORNET BOURDOIS	

A. H. Allenby Lt Col
Comdg R. Sc Fus

Army Form C. 2118.

WAR DIARY
or and 7th Royal Scots Fusiliers
INTELLIGENCE SUMMARY.
(Erase heading not required.)

Instructions regarding War Diaries and Intelligence Summaries are contained in F. S. Regs., Part II. and the Staff Manual respectively. Title pages will be prepared in manuscript.

Place	Date 1915	Hour	Summary of Events and Information	Remarks and references to Appendices
	July			
HAM-EN ARTOIS	16	10.50 pm	Artillery orders to march on the 17th (in Brigade) to HESDIGNEUL	A.H.Q. App XX
HESDIGNEUL	17	2.30 pm	Arrived HESDIGNEUL	
"	18		⎫	
"	19		⎟	
"	20		⎟	
"	21		⎟	
"	22		⎬ Halt (in billets).	
"	23		⎟	
"	24		⎟	
"	25		⎟	
"	26		⎟	
"	27		⎭	
"	28			
"	29			
"	30			
"	31			

A. H. Allenby Col
Comdg. R. Sc. Fus.

15th Division

121/6607

2.F.
Exhibits

7th Royal Scots Fusiliers
Vol: II
From 1 - 31. 8. 15

Army Form C. 2118.

WAR DIARY
or
INTELLIGENCE SUMMARY.
(Erase heading not required.)

Instructions regarding War Diaries and Intelligence Summaries are contained in F. S. Regs., Part II. and the Staff Manual respectively. Title pages will be prepared in manuscript.

Place	Date	Hour	Summary of Events and Information	Remarks and references to Appendices
	1915 August			
HESDIGNEUL	1st	—	Host Billets	
"	2nd	—	"	
"	3rd	5:30pm	Marched from HESDIGNEUL	
PHILOSOPHE	—	9:45pm	Picket and Billets — on relieving the 15th Battalion London Regt. became a Battalion of the Brigade reserve in Section "X"	
"	4	—	Halt	
"	5	—	Half Brigade reserve	10 officers and 390 other ranks employed supporting trenches on right of the 45th Dvn
"	6	—	Half "	12 officers 350 other ranks employed supporting trenches on right of 45th Dvn
"	7	4:30pm	2nd Lt A.H. Allenby hit direct Lieut Morris R.A.M.C. wounded, assault 8th army Medical Pte Denton slightly wounded. 10 officers 350 men employed in improving existing trenches. Battalion in Brigade Reserve. 10 officers 380 employed in improving connecting trenches. Battalion in Brigade Reserve. Colonel A.H. Allenby was buried in MAZINGARBE Cemetery at 8:30 p.m on 8th August — the O.C. 45th Dvn Genl and other officers of other regts of by and attended and other officers in Brigade Reserve	
"	8th to 9th	—	in improving existing trenches. Battalion in Brigade Reserve	
"	9th to 10th	—	in Brigade Reserve. Colonel A.H. Allenby was buried in MAZINGARBE Cemetery at 8:30 p.m on 8th August — the O.C. 45th Dvn Genl and other officers of other regts of by and attended	
"	—	—	10 officers 350 men employed in improving existing trenches. Battalion in Brigade Reserve	
Quality Street	10th	2:30pm	Battalion took over front X.1 from 13th Royal Scots	
"	11th	—	Improvement of trenches. Two patrols not reported enemy's snipers active especially on Sap opposite Boyan S.A. Enemy Helmet Home Y. Signals sent by rocket from direction of MAROC	

1577 Wt. W10791/1773 500,000 1/15 D.D. & L. A.D.S.S./Forms/C. 2118.

Army Form C. 2118.

WAR DIARY
or
INTELLIGENCE SUMMARY.
(Erase heading not required.)

Instructions regarding War Diaries and Intelligence Summaries are contained in F. S. Regs., Part II. and the Staff Manual respectively. Title pages will be prepared in manuscript.

Place	Date	Hour	Summary of Events and Information	Remarks and references to Appendices
QUALITY STREET	12-8-15		Improvement of parapet & parados continued. Trenches A1 & 9 deepened. Sniper on "Beringo" Sap on LENS - CALAIS G.34.C.7.8. reported killed, this Sap has been lengthened out 35 ft. Two German snipers screens found in Sap 18. Quality Street slightly shelled about noon.	
"	13-8-15		Improvement of parapet & parados continued. Enemy sniper working officer J & Sector displaced, working in the old "a fire" trenches. Trench A1 deepened 1 ft. Sap 130 jerks peted 2 rods east. 160 jerks of Jonville reported. German working parties. Very light signals seen at MAROC twice after dark. Fired a Field (German) fired to night of X1 Enemy Field Tramf. No casualties.	
"	14-8-15		Improvement of trenches continued as on 13.8.15. Gallery party under officer J.S. Sections continued with a dug out. Unit on parapet repaired by R.E. Offrs. Used Pistol "A" by out along Sap.18, reported enemy working party out. German sniper located Enemy Sap a LENS road killed by no Whoop at 6.4pm. that was indication of German casualties. Enemy continuing new trench from this Sap to Sap 18.	
"	15-8-15		About working parties R.Scott, J.F. Jackson & R.E. continued small improvement of No trans trenches. Communication trenches constructed. Dug outs improving too trenches & parados. A patrol No.4 by water Scot Priest. 10 N.C.O. & three Rank out to find out if there was enemy snipers returned & Patrol enemy no one. The following casualties received the Parole slightly wounded. Pte Riley Reeve Sgt Maddey slightly wounded to Off Payne slightly wounded	

1577 Wt.W10791/1773 500,000 1/15 D. D. & L. A.D.S.S./Forms/C. 2118.

WAR DIARY or INTELLIGENCE SUMMARY

Army Form C. 2118.

Place	Date	Hour	Summary of Events and Information	Remarks and references to Appendices
QUALITY STREET	16-8-15		Improvement of Trenches continued. Wiring of old support trenches in front of carried out by 13th R. Platoon.	
	17-8-15	1-30 pm	Bayeux deepened & improved. No 10954 Pte Glen accompanied by Capt Turner R.F.A. entered enemy's Saps on LENS-CALAIS road & returned with some valuable information. Pte Glen was wounded about 10.30 p.m. when on listening patrol by the German distanced bomb on wire. Pte Glen's name has been brought to notice of J.O.C. 45th Inf Bde. Very wet.	
"	17-8-15		Captain Stevens slightly wounded in the foot whilst out with a listening patrol. Attack was seen by the enemy & fired upon. Pte Hopkinson A.Coy wounded slightly result of shell fire. "B" Coy reported German who attempted to crawl toward trench from the wire. The men occupied held our fire. Hope our little trench bombing Coys boys away in relief. 3800 bombs thrown, killed & placed in position by the battalion during ? for previous days. To return occupied sector No 1.	
"	18-8-15		Reserved by 45th Inf. Bde Anderson. Work completed at 12 noon.	
LE PHILOSOPHE	18-8-15	1-45 p.m.	Headquarters arrived 1-45 pm. Reserved by 10th Green Skye inters at 7-45 p.m.	
MAZINGARBE	18-8-15			
"	19-8-15		Reported to Bde Headquarters & time arrived & installed as Divisional Reserve at 10 p.m. Working party of 1 officer & 350 men on the GRENAY LINE of communication trenches. Coy officers under Commanding Officer visited LE PREBIE & inspected the GRENAY Line.	

Army Form C. 2118.

WAR DIARY
or
INTELLIGENCE SUMMARY.
(Erase heading not required.)

Place	Date	Hour	Summary of Events and Information	Remarks and references to Appendices
MAZINGARBE	20-8-15		Three officers & 150 men working party in GRENAY-VERMELLES line. Battalion in Divisional Reserve. Nothing of note occurred. Lt Lumsden & 28 men proceeded to school of bombing MOEUX-LES-MINES.	
"	21-8-15		Three officers & 150 men working party in GRENAY-VERMELLES line. 4 officers and 200 men working party in the communication trench Hulks XI. 1 Sergt & 1 Sergeant & 27 men rejoined themselves from q & R Para Families. Sgt Twomey left for hospital at HAVRE injured with the Coys. Visit of B.N. Willoughby. From this have admitted to hospital suffering from casualty of the nose. Weekly state 29 officers 990 other ranks. No other officers include Lieut. Bourne R.A.M.C who is now in hospital at the base as of his trip too two him emergencies Lieut Harris who is now in hospital at the base as of his trip too two him emergencies.	
"	22-8-15		3 officers and 150 men working party in GRENAY-VERMELLES line. The commanding officer (Major W.L. Campbell) & Capt Shipwith accompanied the O.C 20th E Infantry Brigade & staff on a visit to the Bombing school MOEUX-LES-MINES, the new catapult Lent Maurice & Hosta to Trench was explained by Lieut Sampson bombing officer F.E.R. to its Families. Battalion still in Divisional Reserve. The following officers are now known to be in hospital at the base Captain Stevens, Lieut Carde, Lieut Harris R.A.M.C & W.N. Willoughby.	

1577 Wt.W10791/1773 500,000 1/15 D. D. & L. A.D.S.S./Forms/C. 2118.

WAR DIARY
or
INTELLIGENCE SUMMARY.

Army Form C. 2118.

Place	Date	Hour	Summary of Events and Information	Remarks and references to Appendices
MAZINGARBE	23.8.15		3 officers + 150 men working party on GRENAY - VERMELLES line. 4 officers 200 men new communication trench Sector XI. Battalion in Divisional Reserve	
"	24.8.15		3 officers + 150 men working party on GRENAY - VERMELLES line. Battalion received information that it would remain in Divisional Reserve. In an indifferently happy event Corps of Interior in Army sapping & tunnelling under Lt. Col. Becker arranged, 1 N.C.O. + 10 men for Company to attend. Regimental transport closed up to NOEUX-LES-MINES. Battalion to Company.	
"	25.8.15		3 officers + 150 men working party on GRENAY - VERMELLES line. 4 officers 200 men new communication trench Sector XI. Battalion in Divisional Reserve.	
"	26.8.15		8 officers + 400 men employed on a communication trench on X sector under direction of R.E. Battalion. Headquarters visited at 4pm by General Sir Douglas Haig, Commander 1st Army. He was accompanied by O.C. 45th Infantry Brigade (Colonel Trumph). The C.R.E. of Carlisle had Major C.H.S. Hannin, O.C. 9 E. Yorks Rifles had been appointed to the command of the Battalion. Vice Lieut Col M A H Plenty disabled in action.	
"	27.8.15		10 officers and 500 men working on new communication trench - 90% of work completed. Lieut Col C H Y. Heming assumed command of the Battalion.	

WAR DIARY
or
INTELLIGENCE SUMMARY.
(Erase heading not required.)

Army Form C. 2118.

Place	Date	Hour	Summary of Events and Information	Remarks and references to Appendices
MAZINGARBE 2&6				
"	29/8/15		10 Officers and 500 men completed new communication trench —	
Quality Street	30/8/15		10 Officers and 500 men on new reserve trench in 'X' — Relieved Black Watch in sector 'X' — Relief completed by 4.0 p.m. Major E.K. Purnell 2:3rd Northumberland Fusiliers and Major R. Beresford 2:3rd Northumberland Fusiliers joined for 3 days trench instruction; A trench mortar fired a dud on right company of regiment which did not that the shrapnel bullets were fired in stop & caring very thin copper.	
"	31/8/15		There were no working parties; Companies were employed in cleaning and improving their own trenches; Two hostile trench mortars were active at intervals during the day and night;	
"	1/9/15			

Hennin(?) Lieut Col.
Comdg 7th Royal Fusiliers

45th Inf.Bde.
15th Div.

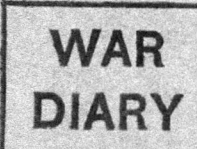

7th BATTN. THE ROYAL SCOTS FUSILIERS.

S E P T E M B E R

1 9 1 5

Attached:

Map.

WAR DIARY or INTELLIGENCE SUMMARY

Army Form C. 2118.

7th R.S.F. September

Place	Date	Hour	Summary of Events and Information	Remarks and references to Appendices
QUALITY STREET	1/9/15		No noticeable parties – Communication trench improvement; scraps dug and loose stone & chalk removed; Majors Beaufort and Purnell left at 7 p.m.; Casualties 2 men killed 3 wounded due to hostile trench mortars; Q.M. Sergt. Fletcher admitted to hospital ruptures while rising a transport horse;	
"	2/9/15		Continued improvement of communication & ambulance dumps; Still very quiet day even in front line completed;	
"	3/9/15		Cellars in quality street prepared for Ambulance; Two men wounded; Battalion Battle Hea Quarters selected.	
	4/9/15		Preparing dugouts for ambulance – Improving battle headquarters – One man wounded; Second North Ammunition arrived –	
	5/9/15		Improving Battalion Battle Head Qrs – Four officers innoculated – attacks for 24 hrs instruction on trenches –	
	6/9/15		Work continued on Battle Head Qrs. Men preparing quality street for ambulance. Sergt Ellens slightly wounded; Received orders to move to NOEUX LES MINES; Relieved from trenches by 7th (Cameron Highlanders) – Relief commences at 6.20 p.m –	
	7/9/15			

Army Form C. 2118.

WAR DIARY or INTELLIGENCE SUMMARY.

(Erase heading not required.)

Instructions regarding War Diaries and Intelligence Summaries are contained in F.S. Regs., Part II. and the Staff Manual respectively. Title pages will be prepared in manuscript.

Place	Date	Hour	Summary of Events and Information	Remarks and references to Appendices
NOEUX LES MINES	7/9/15		Reached NOEUX LES MINES by platoons between 2 am & 3 am:	
" "	8/9/15	8/9/15	Marched from NOEUX LES MINES to LA BEUVRIERE leaving by companies at 2 p.m. arriving at 4.30 p.m : In divisional reserve :	
" "	9/9/15		Cleaned billets. Medical Latrines & inspection of Companies	
" "	10/9/15		Working parties supplied morning and evening 400 men – Bombing class being trained –	
	11/9/15		Routine work :	
	12/9/15		Working party 200 men.	
	13/9/		Routine work – Route march –	
	14/9/		Short scheme & exercise 8.30 to 11 am. Working party 200 mm –.	
	15/9		Working party 60 men & morning 260 at 12 noon . Commanices Coy officers .	
	16/9.		Working party 200 men & 48 officers – Eight Officers went to MAZINGARBE & inspect trenches : Remainder of battalion route march :	
	17/9.		Work under Coy officers – fitting light marching order – occupation of trenches –	
	18/9.		Marching party 140 men 7 h 20'0 – Battalion paraded 9 am & marched in following by occupating trenches – adrnments from same and proceeding overs information	

WAR DIARY or INTELLIGENCE SUMMARY

Army Form C. 2118.

Place	Date	Hour	Summary of Events and Information	Remarks and references to Appendices
LABEUVRIERE	19/9		Church Parade – Inspection of billets – Lieut Burlington went to ST VENANT (?) French motor class.	
"	20/9		Packing kits. Inspection prior in light marching order.	
"	21/9		Sine working parties of 80 men each – Route march by Companies about 8 miles.	
"	22/9		2 Officers & 144 men working party at BETHUNE. Regtl battery formed.	
VAUDRICOURT	23/9		Marched to VAUDRICOURT and Bivouacked in Chateau grounds. Very wet night.	
"	24/9		Left for trenches at 9 pm, marched to GRENAY via and NOEUX and NOUX.	
"	25/9		Left GRENAY line at 4 am & worked up communication trench Southern up in trenches left by 10th Gordons at Quality Street – At 9 am the Battalion advanced on LOOS and meeting with little or no opposition it reached LOOS Village about 10 am. LOOS was cleared and heavy fighting then began for the occupation of Hill 70 beyond it. The Battalion established itself on the crest and dug in. Units being much confused up. The many counter attacks during the night but were repulsed with loss.	The front line of attack left the trenches at 5.30 am
HILL 70	26/9		At 7.30 am a determined that 43rd & B.[?] brenial attack at 9 am preceded by 1 hour bombardment on the Redoubt. This was carried out but owing to the fatigue of the troops and the mixture of units this was unsuccessful. The Battalion held on to its trenches for any the	

WAR DIARY or INTELLIGENCE SUMMARY

Army Form C. 2118.

(Erase heading not required.)

Instructions regarding War Diaries and Intelligence Summaries are contained in F.S. Regs., Part II. and the Staff Manual respectively. Title pages will be prepared in manuscript.

Place	Date	Hour	Summary of Events and Information	Remarks and references to Appendices
	26/9		enemy till 5 pm when they retired & were relieved by the 6th Cavalry Bde – During the day two unsuccessful attacks were made by the 21st Division to join up with our left flank. Casualties during the two days fighting were: Killed 6 Officers 63 men: Wounded 12 Officers 246 men missing 1 Officer 80 men. turn noted that night at Quality Street.	
NOEUX LES MINES	27/9		Marched to MARZINGARBE & noted till 3:30 pm own marched to NOEUX LES MINES & rested the night.	
HAILLICOURT	28/9		marched to HAILLICOURT.	
	29/9		Received capitulating orders from G.O.C. Division & Brigade – At 3 pm the G.O.C. 151st Bde addressed the Battalion & complimented them on their fine work and gallantry displayed in the two days fighting.	
BRUAY	30/9		Left HAILLICOURT at 11:30 am & marched to BRUAY where we went into billets for the night.	
	1/10		marched from BRUAY to LA BUISSIÈRE. Offr. my. the 151st Brigade in addressing Sir Henry Rawlinson Commanding IV Corps complimented & thanked them for their gallant conduct at BEUVRY.	

C. Hemming Lt Col.
Comdg 7th R.S. Fusrs

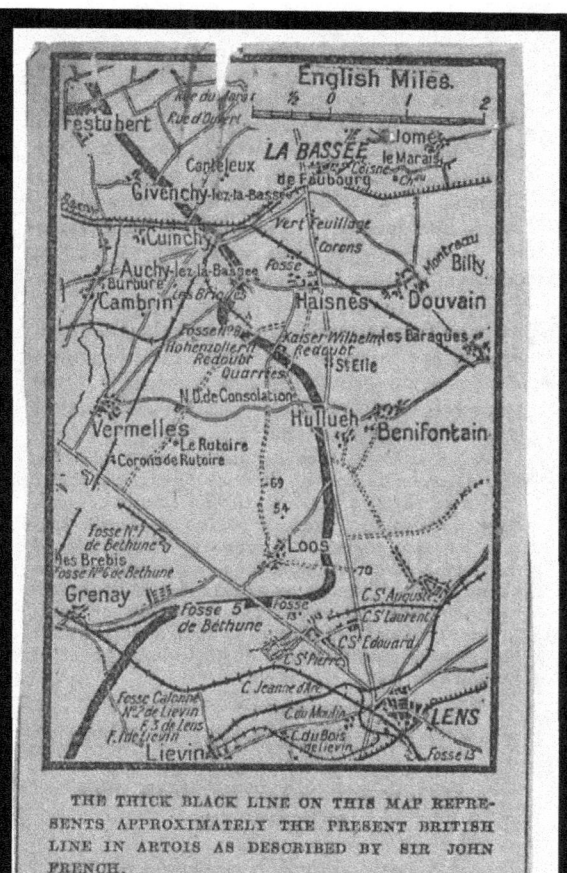

THE THICK BLACK LINE ON THIS MAP REPRESENTS APPROXIMATELY THE PRESENT BRITISH LINE IN ARTOIS AS DESCRIBED BY SIR JOHN FRENCH.

to avoid suspicion of sharing the prevailing sentiment of the country against Germany. They have a reward which some, not without excuse, will say they might have expected from the fellow-nationals of those who bestowed sinister immortality to the phrase 'scrap of paper.' The breaking of their parole by naval officers convinces the average American that the German is not governed by laws which prevail among people of all other civilised nations, and that the German is so lost to all sense of shame and decency that the word of an individual German or the assurance of the German Government means nothing, that a lie is meritorious if it will serve a German's purpose, and any nation that would trust Germany shows its folly."

The *New York World* shows its contempt for the German sense of honour by remarking: "Can it be that there is in the family of civilised nations any member whose war code permits six men together to forswear their personal word of honour as gentlemen, and their professional word of honour as officers, for military advantage, and yet avoid the contempt of their mates in arms? If this is so it is a portent for the serious consideration of the whole world of honourable men."

AMERICA'S DECLINING REVENUE.

PROPOSED EXPORT TAX ON MUNITIONS.

(FROM OUR OWN CORRESPONDENT.)

WASHINGTON, Oct. 20.

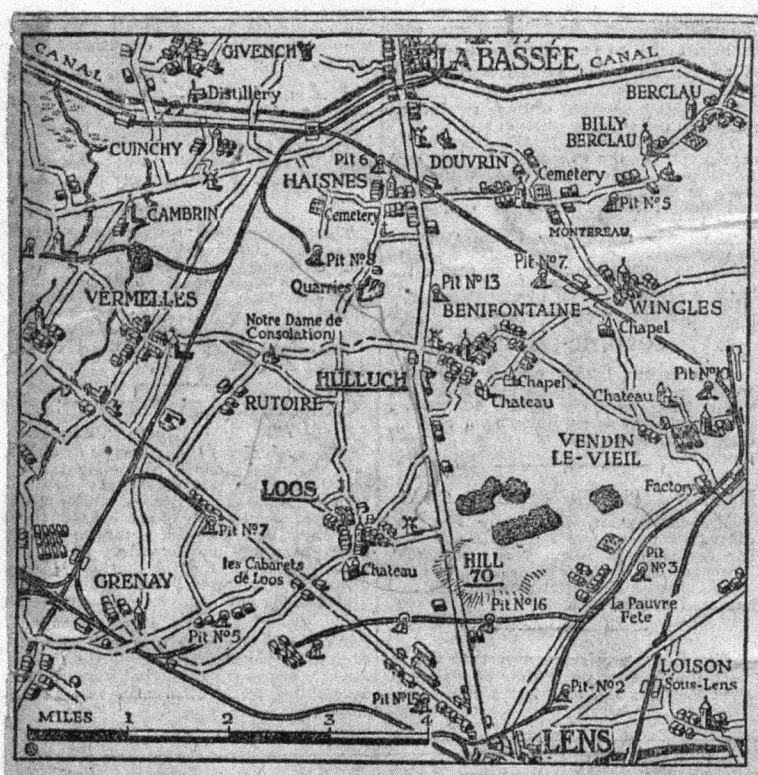

New map of the country between La Bassée and Lens, showing the numerous coal pits near Loos, Hulluch, and Hill 70—the scene of the British advance.

12/7592

15th Known

7th R. Seh Fusilier
Vol 4
Oct 15

H.F.
6 sheets

Army Form C. 2118.

WAR DIARY
7th Royal Scots Fusiliers
INTELLIGENCE SUMMARY.

October 1915

Place	Date	Hour	Summary of Events and Information	Remarks and references to Appendices
BRUAY	1/10/15		Marched from BRUAY to LA BUISSIERE to bivouac there; on the way the 45th Infantry Bde. was addressed by General Sir Henry Rawlinson Commanding IV Corps, congratulated on their gallant conduct and success and thanked for their services.	
LA BUISSIERE	2/10		In Bivouac. The battalion was addressed by Gen. McCracken Comdg. 15th Division and congratulated on their conduct.	
"	3/10		Marched at short notice to billets at ALLOUAGNE	
ALLOUAGNE	4/10		In billets – Refitting battalion.	
"	5/10		—:—	
"	6/10		—:— Lieuts Pirie, Dobbin, Lieut Scott, Manoch, S. Buchan joined the battalion for duty. Lean-granted to Lieut Harr. Thro' throats.	
"	7/10		In fields – Refitting battalion. Lt. Col. Henning & one other rank proceeded on leave	
"	8/10		8 officers & Draft of 70 men joined 2/Lt Hallan proceeded on leave	
"	9/10		2 No officers joined the battalion for duty. Lieut Morrison Bellingham	
"	10/10		1 officer Lieut Carr	
"	11/10			

Army Form C. 2118.

WAR DIARY
or
INTELLIGENCE SUMMARY.
(Erase heading not required.)

Instructions regarding War Diaries and Intelligence Summaries are contained in F. S. Regs., Part II. and the Staff Manual respectively. Title pages will be prepared in manuscript.

Place	Date	Hour	Summary of Events and Information	Remarks and references to Appendices
ALLOUAGNE	13	5.45 PM	Move into billets at HALLICOURT.	
HALLICOURT	14		In Billets in the order to move forward if required. Lieut J. Nelson joined	
"				
MAZINGARBE	15		Move into billets - 2/Lieut Service from 7th Loreen Battalion joined for duty -	
"	16		In billets	
"	17		Officers inspected the trenches about Le Rutoire. 4 Officers & 300 men working party	
"	18		C.O. and Officers inspected trenches SOUTH OF HULLUCH R^d & work again started.	
Sailly	19		Took over C^y SOUTH OF HULLUCH R^d from 7th Sussex.	
"	20		In trenches	
"	21		Heavily shelled 3pm in "Support Trench". A Coy. lost 4 killed & 5 wounded.	
"	22		Relieved in firing line by 13th Royal Scots - Relief started 7pm completed	
		3 am. Moved into Reserve trenches N of HULLUCH R^d	
"	23		In Reserve trench.	
"	24		Move into our British Support trench S of HULLUCH R^d	
"	25		In trenches	
"	26		Moved into billets at NOYELLES. Total Casualties for tour 6 killed & 13 wounded.	

WAR DIARY
or
INTELLIGENCE SUMMARY.

Army Form C. 2118.

Place	Date	Hour	Summary of Events and Information	Remarks and references to Appendices
	October			
NOYELLES	27		Working parties 60 men and 150 men.	
"	28		Jubilee	
"	29		Working party 300 men - 2 Companies bathing at NOEUX.	
"	30		Working party 300 men - Remainder instruction in Gas Helmets & bombing.	
"	31		Church Parade.	

Henry Lt. Col.
Comdg. 7th R.S. Fusiliers.

Jk R.S. Fisher
vol: 5

5 F.
5 sheets

121/7656

15th Kuvairn

Nov 15

Army Form C. 2118.

1st Battalion Royal Scots Fusiliers

WAR DIARY INTELLIGENCE SUMMARY. November 1915.

Place	Date	Hour	Summary of Events and Information	Remarks and references to Appendices
NOYELLES	November 1st		Resting in billets Strength party 150	
"	2nd		" " " 200	
"	3rd		" " Lieut Willoughby (Sutherland) rejoined	
Trenches	4th		Took over from A & S Highlanders	
"	5th		In trenches	
"	6th		In trenches	
"	7th		Relieved in firing line by 13th Royal Scots and became Brigade Support	
"			total casualties 1 killed 2 wounded	
"	8th		In support trenches	
"	9th		" "	
"	10th		" "	
"	11th		Took over Dl Section from A & S Highlanders – the 6th Cameron being on our right and the 6/7 Buffs on our left	
"	12		On this day we had a bombing encounter in the HAIR PIN the enemy shelling the support & communication trenches 245 H.E & shrapnel fell in our area in 4 hours – 1/Pres Wm Fisher 2/Lieut Lockhart & 2 men –	

Army Form C. 2118.

WAR DIARY
or
INTELLIGENCE SUMMARY.
(Erase heading not required.)

Instructions regarding War Diaries and Intelligence Summaries are contained in F. S. Regs., Part II. and the Staff Manual respectively. Title pages will be prepared in manuscript.

Place	Date	Hour	Summary of Events and Information	Remarks and references to Appendices
	November			
Trenches	13		Were relieved by the 9th Black Watch and went into billets at NOEUX —	
NOEUX	14		In billets	
"	15		In billets	
"	16		In billets	
"	17		" " Working party 400 men ..	
"	18		" "	
Trenches	19		In Brigade Support in C' Sector	
"	20		" "	
"	21		Moved into firing line in C'	
"	22		In firing line 2/Lieut Black was killed by a shell —	
"	23		In firing line	
"	24		Moved into Brigade Reserve at NOYELLES — Relieved by 2 Companies of Northampton Regt and 2 Companies of North Lancashire Regt:	
NOYELLES	25		In Reserve	
	26		In Sects C & D having relieved the 13th Royal Scots:	
	27		" " "	
	28		" " "	

WAR DIARY
or
INTELLIGENCE SUMMARY.

Army Form C. 2118.

Place	Date	Hour	Summary of Events and Information	Remarks and references to Appendices
Trenches	November 29th		In Support Trenches C² Lehi	
	30:		" "	
			Extract from the Gazette "No 7512 Sergt. G. J. Williston 7th Battalion Royal Scots Fusiliers: For conspicuous gallantry and ability on Sept 26th 1915 near LOOS. After all the officers had been killed or wounded, Sergeant Williston took command of his company, and his cool bravery contributed greatly to the steadiness of all ranks."	

Clement St Clair
Lt Col
7th R S Fus

Army Form C. 2118.

7th WAR DIARY or INTELLIGENCE SUMMARY.

December 1915

(Erase heading not required.)

Instructions regarding War Diaries and Intelligence Summaries are contained in F. S. Regs., Part II. and the Staff Manual respectively. Title pages will be prepared in manuscript.

6. F.
Infant

Place	Date	Hour	Summary of Events and Information	Remarks and references to Appendices
VERQUIN	1st		Relieve the 8th Seaforths & in minor Reserve	
"	2nd		Cleaning parade;	
"	3rd		Company & battery parade;	
"	4th		200 Working party	
"	5th		300 Working party; 4 Cavalry Officers attached for 6 days	
"	6th		Company Parade: 4 Cavalry	
Trenches	7th		Relieved 8th KOSB's & 10th Scottish Rifles in D1 Section	
"	8th		The Germans showed a parapet & more overlying a friendly nature - There was no apparent intention of surrender though an offer to either a cross to them:	
"	9th		Relieved by 13th Royal Scots & marched to billets at SAILLY LA BOURSE	
SAILLY LA BOURSE	10		Cleaning parade & inspection of feet:	
"	11		Relieve the 13th Royal Scots in D1 Section: Relief complete at 10.15 am	
Trenches	12		In firing line	
"	13		Relieved by 13th Royal Scots and moved into Brigade Support	
"	14		In Brigade Support	

WAR DIARY
or
INTELLIGENCE SUMMARY.
(Erase heading not required.)

Army Form C. 2118.

Place	Date	Hour	Summary of Events and Information	Remarks and references to Appendices
LILLERS	15		Relieved in Bde Support by 22nd London Regt and entrained at NOEUX LES MINES for LILLERS where the 1st Division became Corps Reserve. In rest Billets	
"	16		" " "	
"	17		" " "	
"	18		" " "	
"	19		" " "	
"	20		" en route of Gen French	
"	21		Company drill and training	
"	22		" " "	
"	23		" " "	
"	24		" " "	
"	25		Christmas day	
"	26		Sunday	
"	27			
"	28			

Army Form C. 2118.

WAR DIARY
or
INTELLIGENCE SUMMARY.
(Erase heading not required.)

Instructions regarding War Diaries and Intelligence Summaries are contained in F. S. Regs., Part II. and the Staff Manual respectively. Title pages will be prepared in manuscript.

Place	Date	Hour	Summary of Events and Information	Remarks and references to Appendices
LILLERS	Dec 29		Company training	
	30		" "	
	31		" "	
	1			

Hammersley Lt Col. Indian
1st Royal Scots Fusiliers

Index..........................

SUBJECT.

7th Royal Scots Fusiliers

7. F.

No.	Contents.	Date.
	January 1916	

7th R.S.F. Vol.7

WAR DIARY
or
INTELLIGENCE SUMMARY.

Army Form C. 2118.

JAN. 1916

Place	Date	Hour	Summary of Events and Information	Remarks and references to Appendices
LILLERS	January 1		Company training. Company dinners (holiday)	
	2		Company training. Company dinners (Sunday)	
	3		"	
	4		"	
	5		"	
	6		Divisional Exercise. Billeted in LAIRES.	
	7		"	
	8		Inspection	
	9		Sunday	
	10		Battalion training. Rear guard action	
	11		" Reconnaissance in force	
	12		"	
	13		" Drill	
	14		" Bathing	
	15		Move into Divisional Reserve at MAZINGARBE	
	16		"	

WAR DIARY
or
INTELLIGENCE SUMMARY.

(Erase heading not required.)

Army Form C. 2118.

Place	Date	Hour	Summary of Events and Information	Remarks and references to Appendices
			January 1916.	
MAZINGARBE	17		Bathing	
"	18		Bathing	
"	19		Coy parades	
"	20		Went into front line trenches (Left & right) HULLUCH ROAD relieving 9th & 10th Black Watch 12th H.L.I.	
"	21		In trenches	
"	22		" "	
"	23		Int Brigade Support in O.G.1	
"	24		" "	
"	25		" "	
"	26		" "	
"	27		Moved back into front line as before	
"	28		The enemy attempted after heavy bombardment to break through on our right (10 & SR) — Our machine gun saved the front attack pushed through into Brigade Reserve	
"	29		" " PHILOSOPHE	
"	30		" "	
"	31		" "	

Henry J. Arjunkins
Lt. R.S.

7th R. Scots Fus
15th Div
Vol. 8

44

February 1916

S.F

WAR DIARY
or
INTELLIGENCE SUMMARY.

(Erase heading not required.)

Army Form C. 2118.

Place	Date	Hour	Summary of Events and Information	Remarks and references to Appendices
	February 1916			
NOEUX	1st		In rest billets	
	2d		"	
	3d		"	
	4th		"	
	5th		"	
	6th		"	
	7th		Took over the right of LOOS sector. HILL 70 from 8th R.O.S.B's - D Coy	
			8th R.O.S.B's D Fusiliers attached to us till 13th inst	
Trenches	8th		In trenches front line	
	9th		"	
	10th		"	
	11th		"	
	12th		"	
	13th		Moved back into support line in 10th Avenue relieving R.D Fusiliers	
	14th		In support line	
	15th			

Army Form C. 2118.

WAR DIARY
or
INTELLIGENCE SUMMARY.
(Erase heading not required.)

Place	Date	Hour	Summary of Events and Information	Remarks and references to Appendices
			February 1916	
Tranchée	16		In support line	
"	17		" "	
"	18		" "	
NOEUX	19		Moved into rest billets at NOEUX	
"	20		In billets	
"	21		" "	
"	22		" "	
"	23		" "	
"	24		" "	
"	25		Relieved the 10th Scottish Rifles in 'C' Sector on night of HALLUCH ROAD -
"	26		We exploded a dynamite mine and the crater was occupied. In trenches	
"	27		The Germans sprang a mine about 5:30 pm - we had 22 casualties - no attack was made - 50 yds of parapet was blown in behind which a german trench	
"	28		was dug In trenches	
"	29		In trenches	

Henning Lt
7th R.S.

Index..................

9.F
Schools

SUBJECT.

7th Royal Scots Fusiliers

No.	Contents.	Date.
	March 1916	

Index

Army Form C. 2118.

WAR DIARY
or
INTELLIGENCE SUMMARY.
(Erase heading not required.)

Place	Date	Hour	Summary of Events and Information	Remarks and references to Appendices
			MARCH	
Trenches	1st		In trenches	
"	2nd		Moved into Brigade Support in 10th Avenue	
"	3rd		In Brigade Support	
"	4th		In Brigade Support	
"	5th		Relieved 11th A&S Highlanders in LEFT Sub section of HULLUCH Sector	
"	6th		In trenches	
"	7th		In trenches	
"	8th		Relieved by 7th Camerons and went into billets at MAZIN GARBE	
"	9th		Rest billets	
"	10th		Working parties of 250 men	
"	11th		Billets	
"	12th		Working party 300 men	
"	13th		Billets - MAJOR S.MOTT. left the battalion being appointed D.A.A.Q.M.G. 12th Division	
"	14th		Took over Right Subsection of PUITS 14 BIS Sector from 7th KOSB's	
"	15th		In trenches	
"	16th		In trenches	

WAR DIARY or INTELLIGENCE SUMMARY

Army Form C. 2118.

MARCH

Place	Date	Hour	Summary of Events and Information	Remarks and references to Appendices
Trenches	17th		Relieved by 7th R. Innskillen Fusiliers of XVI Division & moved back into billets at PHILOSOPHE.	
PHILOSOPHE	18th		In billets – Leave reopened.	
"	19th		On night of 19th disposed as follows – 1 Coy PHILOSOPHE, 1 Coy QUALITY STREET, HQ in Old British front line, 2 Coys 10th AVENUE	
Trenches	20		Same as above. Bby moved from QUALITY STREET & GUN TRENCH – a draft of 12 men joined battalion.	
"	21		No change – in trenches –	
"	22		No change	
"	23		Relieved 11th A.& S. Highrs in 14 BIS Right sub sector. HQ near TOSH KEEP.	
"	24		In trenches in LOOS	
"	25		Relieved by 8th Royal Irish – 16th Division – 47th Brigade – Relief completed 10.30 pm & battalion marched to NOEUX.	
NOEUX	26		Battalion entrained at 11.30 am for LA PUGNOY & went into billets there. Capt Clark 13th Royal Regt joined for duty as 2nd in command.	
LA PUGNOY	27		Cleaning parades:	

Army Form C. 2118.

WAR DIARY
or
INTELLIGENCE SUMMARY.
(Erase heading not required.)

Place	Date	Hour	Summary of Events and Information	Remarks and references to Appendices
LAPUGNOY	28		Cleaning Parade	
"	29		Bathing parade at MARLES LES MINES.	
"	30		Platoon and Company drill & route march 1 hour.	
"	31		Musketry at le CHAMP DE TIR and wiring under NCOs of 9th Gordons.	

Clement H A Gourlie
7th R S

Index

SUBJECT.

7th Royal Scots Fusiliers

10 F
7 sheets

No.	Contents.	Date.
	May 1916	
	April	

Army Form C. 2118.

7th R. Scots Fus... Vol IV   15

WAR DIARY
or
INTELLIGENCE SUMMARY.
(Erase heading not required.)

Place	Date	Hour	Summary of Events and Information	Remarks and references to Appendices
LAPUGNOY	April 1	9-12.30	Platoon Drill. 7th R.S.F. in billets. From the Chateau to N.E. end of village. A in Chateau stables. B & Nickey street C on S side of street D up the hill towards the cemetery. Transport named mill. Lewis gunners, Pipers, Scouts etc extreme N.E. end of billets. Captain J.V. Tosh D.S.O. joined from 3rd Bn. Greenock & took over command v/L Col. Hannay who went to hospital. Captain G.W.B. Clark Royal Scots acting as second's command	
	2		Each Coy provide 1 Subaltern & 30 men for instruction in wiring. 3 hours in trench digs. Coys trained under O.C. Coys. Individual training 30+ range in Lewis clan.	
	3.		Wiring Class. Corunna. O.C. Bn. And Shrapnel practice 30 yds range. L Sand Pit. Bois de Dana. And at 101st Chants do Tir.	
	4.		Wiring Class. Musketry. Bathing at Marles les Mines.	
	5.		Wiring Class. Individual Musketry Practices in Sand Pit. Inspection by O.C. of every mans clothing & equipment.	
	6.		Divine at Mans souvenir. Billeted at LICNY LEZ AIRES.	
	7.8.9.		Wiring Class. Bn in anti form etc & Tp. Drill. Individual practices at Sand Pit + Chants de Tir. Major H.C.H. Smith. Com Lorraine arrives Command'g 7 R.S.F.	
	10			

WAR DIARY or INTELLIGENCE SUMMARY

Army Form C. 2118.

7th R. Scots Fusiliers

Place	Date	Hour	Summary of Events and Information	Remarks and references to Appendices
LAPUGNOY	APRIL 11		Wiring. Squads of 2 companies. Cleaning up clothes and equipment.	
	12		Wiring. Squads of 2 companies. Route march. 2 companies musketry on sand pit range. Inter battalion football match.	
	13		Wiring. Squads of 2 coys by day. Squad of 1 coy by night. Bathing parade at Bath MARLES (CAHONNÉ). Bombing squads of 2 coys training. Musketry	
	14		2 coys on range CHAMP de TIR — 40 cartridges in each company. Wiring. Squad of 1 coy in afternoon. Squad of 1 coy at night. Bombing squad of 1 coy training in afternoon. Musketry 2 coys on miniature range. Inspection in afternoon. Outpost scheme in morning. Training S.A.S.	
	15		Wiring. Party of 1 company carrying on ammunition. Inspection of batteries by C.O. Wiring 1 coy afternoon 1 coy at night.	
	16		Bombing training 1 coy afternoon. Church Parade.	
	17		Wiring. 1 coy afternoon 1 coy night. Bombing instruction 1 coy afternoon. Musketry on miniature range in sand pit 2 coys. Bayonet fighting 2 coys in afternoon. Inspection by Sgt. of arms. F. & 10 NCOs received instruction in drill from Sergt. GORNALL 3rd Coldstream Guards	

WAR DIARY or INTELLIGENCE SUMMARY

Army Form C. 2118.

7th R. Scots Fusiliers

Place	Date	Hour	Summary of Events and Information	Remarks and references to Appendices
LAPUGNOY	APRIL 18		Wiring 2 coys by day 1 coy by night. Bombing 2 coys training. Bayonet fighting on Hazeal Coune all companies. Musketry on CHAMP de TIR range 2 coys. Snipers on training range in afternoon 4 men left 6 p.m. 252nd Tunnelling Coy R.E. CHAMP de TIR	
	19		Wiring 2 coy by day 1 coy by night. Bombing 2 coys training. Musketry on Sharpest range (miniature) all companies. Battery parade at MARLES (CALONNE) Inspection of horses by ADVS. 2nd Lt I.G. SMITH joined for duty.	
	20		Wiring 2 coys by day 1 coy at night. Bombing 1 coy training on afternoon. Route March to MARLES – LOZINGHEM – ALLOUAGNE. Lecture by Intelligence Officer 12th Division on left sector of our front at 5 p.m.	
	21		Wiring 1 coy again inspected by GOC 45th Bde. Reported very good. 100 grids long 2 traps wide erected 45 minutes. 9-10 Bayonet fighting training 10.30–11.20 Company drill 11.20–12.20 Battalion drill. Snipers on miniature range conducting loopholes at under 2 ft.	

PETTIGREW. N. Acting Officer

WAR DIARY
or
INTELLIGENCE SUMMARY

Army Form C. 2118.

1 Bn R. Scots Fusiliers

Place	Date	Hour	Summary of Events and Information	Remarks and references to Appendices
LAPUGNOY	APRIL 22		Inspection by G.O.C. 15th DIVISION	
		8.30am	2 Companies will over	
		9.30am	1 Company Coy 1 Platoon Field Service Marching Order	
		10.15am	1 Platoon musketry 2 sections rapid 2 sections grouping	
		11.15am	Bombing Jenkins 1 company in attack. Wiring Party same company constructing wire 100 yards long 2 bags wide. Time taken 40 minutes	
		12 noon	Machine guns and limbered wagons NCO's (10) turned out in drill order. Sergt GORNALL 2nd Colhoun Thanks. Knowledge	
	23		Church Parade. Report received from A.D.V.S. "The Transport animals are in excellent condition no signs of skin disease among them and they are evidently well cared for."	
	24		Brigade Route March to RAIMBERT to various anvils demonstration Coat Machine on 2LT A.M. GRIFFE for developing Battery Boils Order No 674 acted taken no 3rd of man is permitted to be in possession of a camera. 2LT D.C. BROWN joined for duty	

Army Form C. 2118.

7th R. Scots Fusiliers

WAR DIARY
or
INTELLIGENCE SUMMARY.
(Erase heading not required.)

Instructions regarding War Diaries and Intelligence Summaries are contained in F. S. Regs., Part II. and the Staff Manual respectively. Title pages will be prepared in manuscript.

Place	Date	Hour	Summary of Events and Information	Remarks and references to Appendices
	APRIL			
LAPUGNOY	25		Bugle Sports. 2Lt BOYLE joined for duty	
	26		Cleaning up billets	
	27		Marched by road to billets in BETHUNE starting at 8am. Just before starting gas which had been sent over at LOOS reached LAPUGNOY but was only then strong enough to draw tears to the eyes. Reconnoitred Defence Positions in VERMELLES & NOYELLES	
BETHUNE	28		Parades under O.C. Companies	
	29		Smoke Helmet practice all companies. Bombing practice all coys. Physical drill	
	30		Divine Service	
	~~29~~ 1st MAY		Physical training 1 hour. Smoke helmet drill 1 hour. Bombing practice 1 hour. Bayonet fighting 1 hour. Bathing 2 coys	
	2		Physical training, Smoke helmet practice, Bombing practice, Bayonet fighting and Baths 2 coys as on 1st	
	3		Battalion moved into reserve trenches. Headquarters VERMELLES	
VERMELLES	4		In reserve trenches. Quiet. Working Party to Royal Scots & R.E.	
	5		In reserve trenches. Quiet	— do —

www.ingramcontent.com/pod-product-compliance
Lightning Source LLC
Chambersburg PA
CBHW081455160426
43193CB00013B/2487